DIGGING DEEPER INTO THE PAST

THE VIKINGS

JOHN AND LOUISE JAMES

Heinemann
LIBRARY

ACKNOWLEDGEMENTS

First published in Great Britain in 1998
by Heinemann Library,
Halley Court, Jordan Hill, Oxford, OX2 8EJ,
a division of Reed Educational & Professional Publishing Ltd.

OXFORD MELBOURNE AUCKLAND
JOHANNESBURG BLANTYRE GABORONE
IBADAN PORTSMOUTH (NH) USA CHICAGO

Written by: Louise James **Illustrated by**: John James
Editor: Andrew Farrow **Design**: John James and Alec Slatter

02 01 00 99 98
10 9 8 7 6 5 4 3 2 1

ISBN 0 431 07176 4

A CIP catalogue record for this book is available from the British Library.
This title is also available in a hardback library edition (ISBN 0 431 05323 5).
Printed and bound in Italy

The publishers would like to thank Dr Richard Hall of York Archaeological Trust
for his advice and assistance in the preparation of this book, and the organizations
that have given their permission to reproduce the following pictures:

Ancient Art and Architecture Collection: 9 (warrior ship).
Arnamagnaean Institute, Copenhagen: 25 (parchment), 26 (book), 28 (book).
ATA, Sweden: 23 (glassware).
Bergen Museum: 12 (smoothing board).
Courtesy of the Trustees of the British Museum: 7 (coin).
C. M. Dixon/Photoresources: 13 (oval brooch), 18 (panel).
Werner Forman Archive: 9 (coin), 20 (axe), 24 (mould).
Galve Museum: 22 (brazier).
Historical Museum, Moesgard, Denmark: 19 (bellows stone).
Michael Holford: 9 (men in boat), 10 (Bayeux Tapestry).
Knudsens Photocenter: 12 (cauldron), 15 (sickle), 18 (knife), 20 (swords).
National Museum of Antiquities, St Germain-en-Laye: 20 (arm ring and buckle).
National Museum of Antiquities of Scotland, Edinburgh: 13 (cloak brooches and rings).
National Museum of Copenhagen: 24 (altar piece), 26 (gaming piece), 29 (arrow head).
National Museum of Ireland: 11 (ship graffito), 26 (gaming board).
Parks Canada, Canadian Heritage: 28 (ring pin).
The Pierpont Morgan Library/Art Resource, New York M.736, f.9v: 8 (Invasion of the Danes).
State Historical Museum, Sweden: 20 (warrior), 21 (runestone), 22 (purse), 25 (Freya and Thor pendants).
State Historical Museum/ATA, Sweden: 11 (wind vane).
Stofnun Arna Magnussonar, Iceland: 5 (*Flateyjarbok*).
Trondheim Museum: 10 (plank).
Universitetets Oldsaksamling, Oslo: 23 (amber beast).
York Archaeological Trust: 5 (locks and X-ray), 13 (round brooch),
16 (comb, pins and weights), 17 (coin die and coins), 23 (coin).

Every effort has been made to contact copyright holders of any material reproduced in this book.
Any omissions will be rectified in subsequent printings if notice is given to the Publisher.

CONTENTS

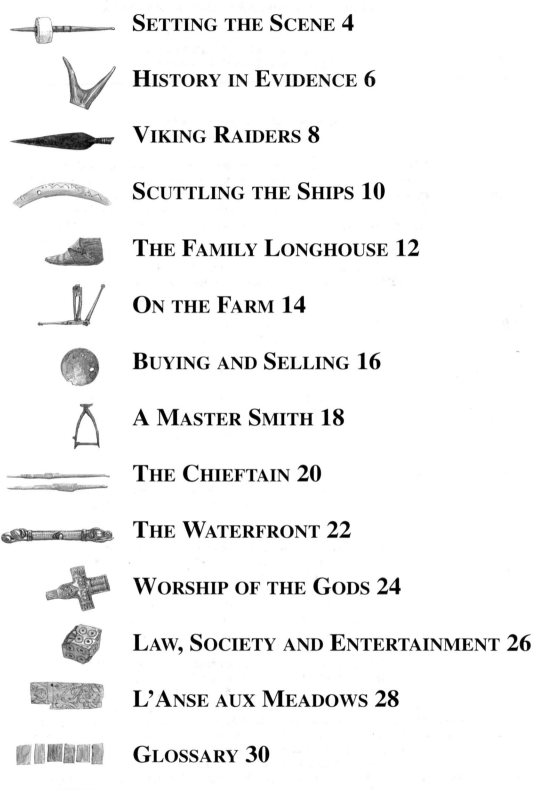

Setting the Scene

EUROPE, CIRCA AD 780-1070

The Vikings, or Norsemen as they are often called, came from the northern countries of Sweden, Norway and Denmark. They dominated much of northern Europe between the 8th and 11th centuries. They were excellent sailors and talented craftsmen who traded in many lands, earning great wealth. Some journeyed as far as the Middle East, and others sailed to the American continent. Some Vikings used their great skill in sailing to attack their neighbours.

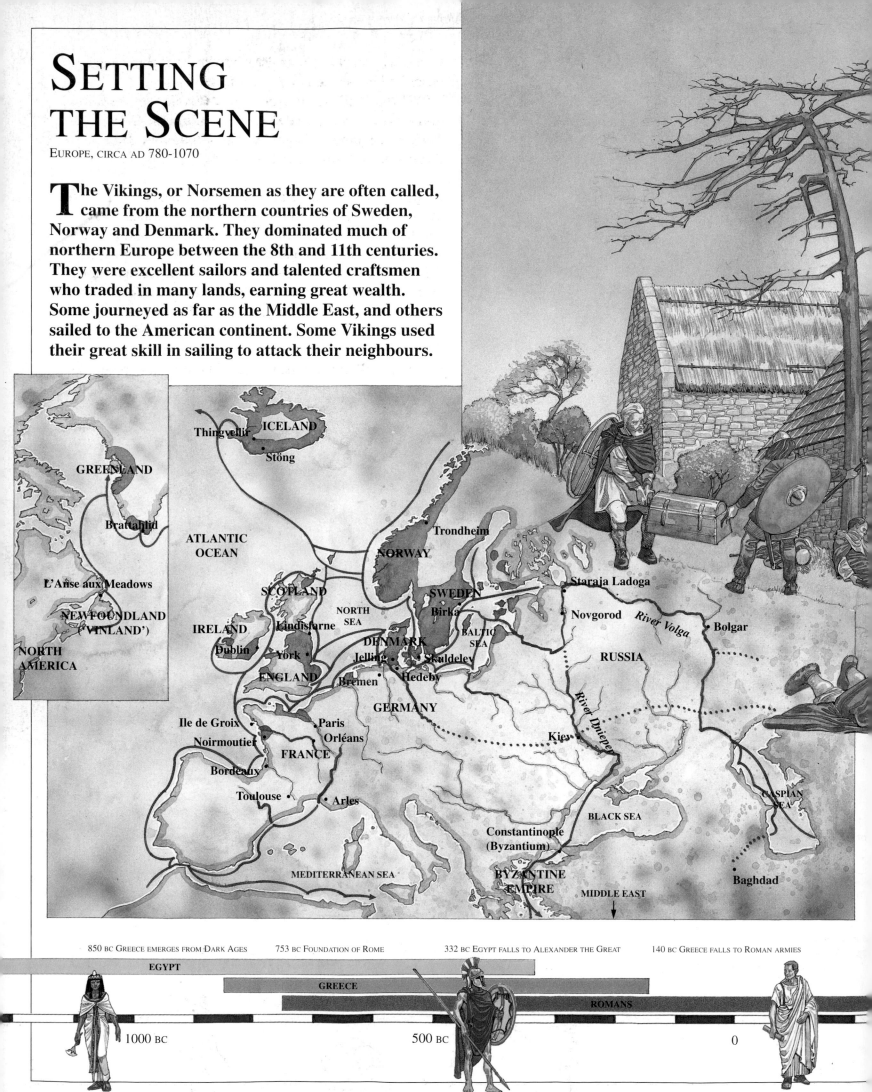

GREENLAND

Brattahlid

ATLANTIC OCEAN

L'Anse aux Meadows

NEWFOUNDLAND ('VINLAND')

NORTH AMERICA

Thingvellir ICELAND
Stöng

SCOTLAND

IRELAND
Dublin
York
ENGLAND

Lindisfarne

NORTH SEA

NORWAY Trondheim

SWEDEN
Birka

DENMARK
Jelling Skuldelev
Hedeby

Staraja Ladoga

Novgorod River Volga Bolgar

BALTIC SEA

RUSSIA

GERMANY

Bremen

Ile de Groix Paris
Noirmoutier Orléans
FRANCE
Bordeaux

Toulouse Arles

Kiev

River Dnieper

MEDITERRANEAN SEA

BLACK SEA

Constantinople (Byzantium)

BYZANTINE EMPIRE

MIDDLE EAST

CASPIAN SEA

Baghdad

850 BC GREECE EMERGES FROM DARK AGES   753 BC FOUNDATION OF ROME   332 BC EGYPT FALLS TO ALEXANDER THE GREAT   140 BC GREECE FALLS TO ROMAN ARMIES

EGYPT

GREECE

ROMANS

1000 BC   500 BC   0

One Christian churchman, Ermentarius of Noirmoutier, described raids made by the Vikings in France:

'862 AD. The Vikings over-run all that lies before them, and none can withstand them. They seize Bordeaux, Periguex, Limoges, Angoulême and Toulouse. Angers, Tours and Orléans are made deserts.'

As time passed, Vikings also began to settle, or live in, some of the other countries in Europe, including France, Britain and Ireland. There they married the local men and women, and even adopted some of their way of life.

This book looks at a selection of the evidence that shows us what the Vikings were like. This evidence includes tools, weapons and household objects, as well as stories called sagas and church records from the Viking period. Using the fascinating discoveries that archaeologists have made, historians can unravel the mystery of our past, to reveal so much about the Viking way of life...

Main areas of settlement

Sea and river routes

Main overland trade routes

The map (left) shows the main areas of Viking activity, from Greenland to Constantinople. The inset map shows how the Vikings might have sailed to Newfoundland from Greenland.

The scene above shows a popular view of the Vikings. A band of fierce warriors is raiding a monastery, killing monks or taking them as prisoners, and seizing valuable goods before returning to their sleek 'dragon ships'. What evidence is there that the Vikings were like this?

The timeline below shows how the 'Viking Age' (which lasted from about AD 780 to 1070) fits into world history.

AD 780 FIRST MAJOR VIKING RAIDS

AD 1070 END OF VIKING AGE

AD 1517 BEGINNING OF THE REFORMATION

AD 476 ROME FALLS

AD 1250 AZTECS SETTLE IN VALLEY OF MEXICO

AD 1521 FALL OF AZTECS

MIDDLE AGES

VIKINGS

AZTECS

AD 500

AD 1000

AD 1500

HISTORY IN EVIDENCE

Much of our evidence about the Vikings has been discovered by archaeologists and historians. In many ways they are like detectives, finding clues and piecing together the evidence until they form a picture of how people lived. Sometimes these clues do not provide a complete picture, so we have to make intelligent guesses about how people dressed or how they did things.

Archaeological sites can provide evidence about historical buildings, from the Celtic round hut (bottom) to a modern tower block (top).

750   850   950

Dendrochronology is an accurate method of dating wood. For each year that a tree grows, it forms a growth ring. By overlapping and matching these rings (above), it is possible to produce a calendar of rings that can be used to date other pieces of wood.

An archaeological dig is in progress (right), uncovering important remains, perhaps from the Viking period. Working through the layers of soil and old buildings, the team of archaeologists will carefully record the details and positions of any remains and artefacts they find.

Archaeologists study all the places where people have left their mark – their homes, farms, temples, cemeteries and places of work. They investigate layers of earth to find traces of how people in the past lived. Before 'digging' begins, accurate records of a site are made. Special resistivity and magnetic surveys might be used to indicate the presence of underground features, such as a ditch or stone wall.

As the site is 'dug', all the items that are found are recorded, labelled and sent to experts for preservation and study. Often it is possible to reconstruct individual objects: for example, pieces of pottery can be reassembled to show the shape and size of the original vessel.

Any soil taken from an excavation is sifted thoroughly to check that small artefacts have not been missed. Microscopic examination of soil can also show what type of plants grew in it, what animals grazed on the land, and even the food that people ate.

Here are some of the tools an archaeologist uses, from a metric measuring pole, a tape measure and a bucket to carry away soil, to a drawing board and a lap-top computer for recording finds and writing reports.

A coin can help to date a site. However, the coin could accidentally have been buried lower (eg by ploughing) or higher (by being lost later) than its date would suggest.

Runestones, tall standing stones, are inscribed with runes and simple pictures. This large runestone commemorates a Viking farmer who had visited Jerusalem and died in Greece.

Sometimes an old metal object (left) is so badly corroded that it is difficult to tell what it is. Here an X-ray photo of the object has been taken, revealing that it is a lock. Now an archaeological conservator will know exactly what he or she is trying to clean and restore.

This illuminated manuscript, called the Flateyjarbok, *tells of the exploration of Vinland (see* page 28). *It is one of a series of Viking stories called sagas. These were meant to entertain people, so storytellers probably made the events in them seem more exciting than they really were.*

Viking Raiders

In the 9th and 10th centuries, the people of western Europe suffered terrifying attacks by bands of Viking warriors. These fierce raiders took any objects they thought would be useful or valuable. They also seized people to sell as slaves, or to hold for ransom. There were two main reasons for the Vikings' success. Firstly, they were fierce warriors who seemed to have no fear of death. Secondly, they had superb warships called longships. Alcuin, an English churchman, described how Viking kings and chieftains commanded a terrifying power.

'...*never before has such terror appeared in Britain as we have now suffered from a pagan race, nor was it thought that such an inroad from the sea could be made.*'

Viking warships were called 'dragon ships' by people who saw the fierce wooden figureheads on their prows. No dragon prow has survived, but the picture on the right shows how one might have looked.

Evidence for what ship figureheads looked like includes Viking graffiti (left) and iron ornaments from the Ladby ship (below left).

The rowers would have used a wooden bailer (left) to scoop water out of the boat. Several oars (below) were found with the Ladby ship.

The picture on the left is called 'Invasion of the Danes'. It is from a religious history illustrated in about 1130. Vikings often raided the wealthy monasteries, which owned many beautiful and valuable religious treasures. Hundreds of monks were killed, and others were taken to be ransomed (see also page 23).

The coin below was minted in the city of Hedeby, which was then in Viking-Age Denmark but is now part of Germany. It shows a Viking ship with a sail and high prow and stern post.

The Ladby ship was found in a large earth burial mound (left). None of its planks have survived, but scientists have been able to work out its shape from the impressions it left in the soil.

These carved stones from Sweden show two Viking ships with sails and warriors inside. They are evidence of how Viking ships were probably rigged. Archaeologists did not find a mast or sail with the Ladby ship, but there were four iron rings on each side where the rigging was tied.

Beautifully designed, the sleek Viking longships were built of overlapping planks that enabled them to flex (bend) in rough seas. They also had a low draught, and so could sail in very shallow water. Not only did raiders attack coastal settlements, they raided far inland, rowing many kilometres upriver to surprise their victims. Even the cities of Paris and Kiev were attacked by Viking armies.

The ship in the scene is based on one found at Ladby in Denmark. It is about 21m long but only 3m wide and 0.65m deep! Although she has a mast and sail, her crew will only use them in open water and in good weather. She is here being rowed up a narrow river. In her stern, one of the crew is using a steering oar (right) to guide the ship. If the boy on the bank runs ahead with a warning, the raiders will lose their advantage of surprise.

SCUTTLING THE SHIPS

DENMARK AD 1100

It has always been difficult to sail up the fiord at Skuldelev near Roskilde in Denmark. There was only a narrow, shallow channel which boats could pass through without running aground. Then, in 1957, archaeologists who were working under the water discovered why: the fiord had been blocked by the wrecks of five ships. The remains – over 1,500 large pieces of wood – have provided some of the best evidence of what Viking vessels were really like.

Two were warships. One was about 18m long and built of oak and ash. She was narrow and shallow like the Ladby ship, and could easily have landed Viking warriors on a beach. The other was about 28m long with over 25 oars each side. It was so big it probably needed to dock at a harbour. It must have belonged to a powerful chieftain.

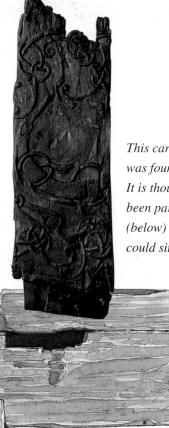

This carved plank was found in Norway. It is thought to have been part of a chest (below) that rowers could sit on.

Left is a scene from the Bayeux Tapestry. It depicts Norman craftsmen, who were descended from the Vikings, building boats. The men can clearly be seen using a variety of tools to shape and smooth the wood. Marks made by tools can sometimes be seen on the remains of boats.

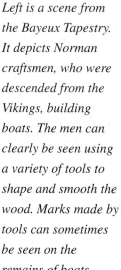

Archaeologists have found many of the tools used for boat-building, including axe heads, and scrapers for shaping the wood.

The remains of the ships can tell us many things. The ocean-going cargo ship has marks that show it was once hit by an arrow! The plank above comes from the big warship shown in the centre of the main scene. Using dendrochronology, scientists discovered that this huge vessel was made in Ireland in about 1060.

In 1961, a metal dam was built around the five Skuldelev ships (right). The water was pumped out and the remains removed for further study.

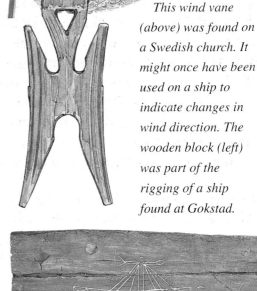

This wind vane (above) was found on a Swedish church. It might once have been used on a ship to indicate changes in wind direction. The wooden block (left) was part of the rigging of a ship found at Gokstad.

Sailors filled the ships with rocks to make the blockade stronger (left). Long wooden poles were also used to hold the scuttled vessels in place.

This 11th-century wooden plank was found in Ireland. The ship sketched on it has a dragon prow, sails and perhaps a wind vane.

The Vikings also used ships for trading as well as raiding. One of the wrecks was a large merchant vessel called a knarr, like the one on the right of the scene. It could have sailed across the oceans, carrying as much as 25 tonnes of cargo, including large animals such as horses and cows. A replica of the fourth vessel, a smaller cargo boat, has been built. People have been able to sail her at 8-9 knots. The fifth wreck was a small fishing boat. It was probably used to fish for herring in the fiord.

Why did the Vikings decide to block the entrance to Roskilde? We can only guess. Perhaps the people of Roskilde did it to defend themselves from attacks by another Viking chieftain.

THE FAMILY LONGHOUSE

NORWAY AD 1050

Most Vikings lived in family homes called longhouses. The longhouse was a large, low rectangular building with one main room, which had a hearth in the centre. In the hearth burned a fire which gave light and heat to the rest of the home. There were no chimneys in Viking homes, so smoke from the fire had to escape through a small hole in the roof.

Family life centred around the fire. The women in the family prepared and cooked the food, before the whole family ate while sitting around the hearth. At night everyone slept on beds along the sides of the longhouse.

Women were expected to do all the household chores. Girls were taught to spin wool and flax. This they then wove on a loom (shown to the right of the scene) to make cloth. The cloth was used to clothe the family, but could also be sold or bartered (see pages 16-17).

This whalebone plaque (right) is probably an ironing board. The glass ball is flat on one side: when heated it was used as an iron.

On the left are some everyday wooden and metal utensils. The rectangular platter was used in cheese-making. The long-handled dish would have been used for baking food over the fire.

This bowl is carved out of soapstone, a soft natural rock found in Norway and the Shetland Islands.

Valuable items like the copper cauldron (below) belonged to important, wealthy families. This one was found in a woman's grave in Norway.

An archaeologist carefully uncovers the stones of a hearth (above). Within the remains of the fire there might be traces of the food that had been cooked. Also visible are some of the holes for the wall posts and perhaps where the loom stood.

This Viking woman is wearing her best clothes. The Vikings liked bright colours and jewellery. The child is wearing a pendant representing the hammer of the god Thor (see page 25).

Embroidery was another important craft. Wealthy Vikings bought huge tapestries to hang on the walls of their homes. These were both to decorate their homes and keep out cold draughts.

As well as being draughty, the hygiene in homes was poor as the Vikings knew nothing of microscopic germs. Water supplies often became contaminated because toilets (which were just holes in the ground) were often dug close to the streams and wells. If people became ill there were no doctors or surgeons, only a few simple medicines made from herbs. So people often died young.

These brooches (left and below left) could be worn by women as fasteners (to hold up an apron) and as decoration. A Moorish traveller named Al-Tartushi also described Viking woman as 'enhancing their beauty with artificial make-up'.

The two large brooches (below) would have been worn by men and sometimes women to fasten their cloaks. Bottom left are three small arm rings.

Making cloth was an important job for the women. Here are a wooden spindle used in spinning, weights used on the loom, and a comb to prepare wool for spinning.

ON THE FARM

ICELAND AD 1103

Most Vikings lived on farms, growing crops and raising animals. A nobleman or free man probably owned his own land and farm. If a farm was large then there were usually slaves to do the hard and dirty work. Some slaves were Vikings, while others were people who had been captured on raids.

Farmers had only simple wooden and metal tools to till the soil and prepare it for crops. In places where crops flourished, farmers could grow corn, barley or oats. These were used for making bread and beer. Other crops included vegetables such as cabbages, peas and turnips. The Vikings also collected honey to sweeten their drinks, and wild fruit and berries to eat and to use as dyes for cloth.

This quern, for grinding grain, was found on the site of a Viking farm in England. It is typical of querns used by Vikings to make flour. Grain was ground between the stones by turning a wooden handle in a hole in the top stone.

The archaeological dig above shows a farm at Stöng in Iceland. The remains of the farm have been preserved under volcanic ash from Mount Hekla, which erupted in 1104. The building had stone foundations and turf walls and roofs.

During the Viking Age, farmers were able to grow plenty of food. There was little risk of starvation and families began to get bigger. Eventually, the Vikings had to look for new land to grow food on. So, not only did the Vikings raid and plunder, they also settled on new land to farm it for themselves. In 874, the first settlement was set up in Iceland, where there was plenty of land for all. The scene (left) shows a farmhouse at Stöng in Iceland.

However, farming in places like Iceland was not easy as the soil was light and stony. This meant that farmers found it easier to keep animals rather than sow large fields of crops. They raised cows and goats for their milk, meat and hides. Sheep provided wool and meat. Many families also kept ducks, geese, chickens and pigs, and also hunted birds and animals for food and hides.

Farmers used tools like these sickles for harvesting, and the wooden spade found by archaeologists in England (below). At Stöng there was a small smithy where tools could be made and repaired.

The farm at Stöng was some distance from the sea. However, many Vikings would have caught fish with hooks like these to supplement their diet. The fresh fish could be cooked, but also preserved by drying or smoking.

Farmers did not have heavy ploughs to turn the soil. Above is a metal tip for an ard, which was pushed through the soil to break it up so seeds could be planted.

On the right are a sharp axe for cutting wood and shears for shearing sheep.

BUYING AND SELLING

BRITAIN AD 975

Some of the goods produced on the farms found their way to Viking towns, where they were sold or swapped for other things. One such town was York, or Jorvik as it was known in Viking times, which was a large and important market town. There, archaeologists have excavated a site, in a street called Coppergate. Using some of the many artefacts found, we have reconstructed the busy market street, shown in the scene on the right, as it might once have existed.

Pieces of deer antler and walrus ivory were found at York. Bone and antler were carved into items like combs, spindle whorls and pins (bottom).

This unusual artefact (above) is the handle of a saw used by a craft worker for sawing antler. The decorated handle, itself made of antler, would have had a toothed metal blade.

There have been many exciting finds at York. The earth is permanently damp so many leather and wooden items have been preserved.

We know that crafts such as leather working and bone carving were common. Craft workers sold their goods for silver, or bartered (exchanged) them for something else they wanted. The prices of goods were probably not fixed as they are today, but the buyers and sellers negotiated the price. If the goods exchanged in barter were not of equal value, then the difference had to be made up with silver.

A coin maker could cheat by using a cheaper metal, but it would not be the same weight as silver! These folding scales were used by traders to test the weight of coins.

These coins, known as pennies, were made using a metal stamp called a die (left). One of the coins (far left) has been cut into a quarter by a trader.

Silver coins were used for their weight rather than their face value. Sometimes only a small amount of silver was needed, so the coins, which were quite soft, might be cut into half or fractions. Many traders would carry a small pair of portable scales so they could check the weight of the silver. Most people also made sure a coin was pure silver by making a small nick or 'peck mark' into it with a sharp knife.

Right are some metal spikes called awls. They were used by leather workers to make holes through leather so it could be stitched to make shoes or pouches, for example.

This leather boot (left) is one of many leather items to have been discovered at York. It is well preserved and its stitching and fastener can clearly be seen.

A MASTER SMITH

BRITAIN AD 930

The Vikings were skilled craftsmen. We know that there were many different trades, such as bone and antler carving, while leather workers made shoes and boots and goldsmiths made fine jewellery. Glass workers, who recycled old glass or sometimes made new glass, fashioned colourful beads used for decoration.

However, the most important craftsman in the community was the blacksmith. His work would be used by everyone. He made iron objects such as cooking pots, tools, chains and nails, as well as weapons such as knives and swords. Some smiths had their own workshops, or smithies, while a few travelled from farm to farm with their tools. A smithy was a hot and sooty place, the air thick with smoke. We know that skilled smiths were important men and enjoyed rich rewards because their tools have been found in wealthy burials.

Most tools were for heavy work, like the hammers (right). The heaviest were used for welding and forging, the lighter for delicate work.

Plate shears (above left) were used for cutting sheet metal. The smith would use tongs (above) to hold the red hot iron while he hammered it into shape on his anvil.

This woodcarving from a 12th-century church in Norway shows two heroes of Viking mythology. They are forging a sword on an anvil while using bellows to make the fire hotter. Even the gods thought that a smith's work was important!

Smiths could make a wide range of items, from simple knife blades (above) to complicated locks (see page 7).

The smith in the picture is making a sword, assisted by a young boy who is using bellows to keep the furnace as hot as possible. The sword will become a Viking man's prized possession.

Sword blades were sometimes made by a technique called pattern welding. Iron rods were heated, twisted around each other and then forged together to give a strong but flexible blade. The edges were sharpened and sometimes made even harder by more hammering. Finally, an ornate hilt and grip were fitted. A typical sword was about 80 centimetres long, and would be used to slash at an enemy.

This carved stone would have protected the smith's bellows from the heat of the fire. The hole in the mouth is for the bellows' nozzle.

As well as weapons, smiths made items such as locks and these ornate keys. As there were no banks, many Vikings kept their most valuable possessions, such as their silver and jewellery, locked in wooden chests.

In Viking cities like Hedeby and York, archaeologists have found many workshops. Evidence for metalworking includes signs of hearths and the waste materials used by the craftsmen.

THE CHIEFTAIN

FRANCE AD 930

Chieftains were the local Viking leaders. They led bands of many warriors. Some of these warriors were full-time soldiers who might be away from home for over 20 years. Most were men who lived with their families, but during the summer, between the spring sowing and the autumn harvest, went raiding or trading with their chieftain.

Warriors fought bravely as they did not fear dying. The Christian emperor of the Byzantine Empire was so impressed by the fierce Vikings that he employed some of them in his bodyguard, called the Varangian Guard.

These swords are typical of a warriors' weapons. The gold ring and buckle come from the burial of a chieftain on the Ile de Groix, in France.

Chieftains could afford weapons of the highest quality, such as this spearhead with silver inlaid hilt, and axe with an animal design also inlaid in silver.

Some Vikings were buried with their riding equipment, such as this iron stirrup from Denmark.

This silver pendant shows a Viking warrior on his horse.

Viking weapons included swords, axes, spears and a wooden shield and leather cap. A wealthy warrior or chieftain would probably also have protective chain mail and a metal helmet. Most warriors were men, but the sagas also tell of one woman warrior, called Freydis. She was the daughter of Eric the Red, a famous Viking (see page 28). Freydis led her own band of men, but was shunned when she murdered a group of women and children.

Many Vikings were killed in battle, too. In the scene on the left, a band of Vikings tries to shelter behind their shields as their chieftain lies dying in front of them. Have they been defeated by other Vikings, or by enemies in a foreign land? On the Ile de Groix in France, a Viking chieftain was given a lavish burial. Many warriors were buried with their armour, swords and other possessions. If they owned a horse, this might be slaughtered and buried with them.

The runestone shown below is in Gotland, Sweden. It is thought to represent a dead warrior riding to Valhalla, a place where the gods allow warriors who died bravely to live again (see page 24). The figure below the horse seems to be wearing chain mail.

THE WATERFRONT

DENMARK AD 989

We have seen on pages 16 and 17 how Vikings bought and sold goods from their own lands, such as walrus ivory and skins. They also traded items bought or stolen abroad, and slaves that they had captured on raids. Some merchants even brought home exotic goods produced in distant foreign lands, such as silk, glassware, wine, spices and silver.

We know that the Vikings travelled far to trade, and also that people travelled to Viking ports from places such as the Middle East. One Russian history describes a trade route from the Baltic to the Black Sea, along which lay the great Russian towns of Kiev, Novgorod and Staraja Ladoga. Artefacts found in the two now-deserted ports of Hedeby (Germany) and Birka (Sweden) have helped us to understand the great extent of trade that was carried on.

This fragment of an Indian lizard skin purse (left) was discovered in Sweden. It was perhaps taken there by traders who travelled up the Volga or Dnieper rivers.

Below is a superbly decorated bronze bucket from Ireland, found in Sweden. It could show that Vikings in Sweden and Ireland traded widely with each other, or it could be loot from a raid.

This bronze brazier, possibly from Baghdad, was discovered in Sweden in 1943. It was found hidden beneath a rock. It is thought to have been traded by Arab merchants, and may have been bought and sold many times on its journey.

This piece of thick rope, which was preserved in wet ground in England, would have been used by sailors to tie up their boats.

The Vikings brought back many silver coins, called dirhams, from the Middle East. This one, found in England, is a forgery of a coin from Asia (see page 17).

Amber was prized for use in jewellery. It was delicately carved into small ornaments and beads. Above are a small 'gripping beast' and trinkets from Denmark.

This archaeological dig shows a stream leading down to the waterfront. Because the soil is very damp, many artefacts dropped or lost in the harbour mud will not have perished.

Glass was imported as the Vikings did not usually make glass, only heat and shape it. Right are pieces of glass imported as raw material, and some beads. Below are glass gaming pieces, and drinking glasses from the Rhineland, in Germany.

The scene above is based on a variety of evidence. In 975, a Moorish traveller named Al-Tartushi, who had visited the port of Hedeby, wrote an account of his travels. He said that 'the town is poorly provided with property or treasure. The inhabitants' principal food is fish', and he saw how 'anyone who slaughters an animal by way of sacrifice has a pole outside his house door and hangs the sacrificed animal there'.

The first slave leaving the ship seems to be a monk. Perhaps he will be returned to his monastery in return for money. Most of what we know about the slave trade comes from written accounts; there is little evidence of slave chains or manacles to show that the trade occurred.

The glassware shown here was found in a burial at Birka in Sweden.

23

WORSHIP OF THE GODS

Denmark AD 975

The first Vikings were pagans, worshipping many gods and goddesses. The most important god was Odin. He represented age, wisdom and power. He lived in a magnificent hall called Valhalla, and any Viking warrior who died bravely in battle could go to live there with Odin. Odin's daughter Freya was the goddess of fertility, beauty and love. Another god, Thor, controlled the wind, rain, thunder and lightning.

The Vikings believed that when they died they would live again in another world. So, with great care, dead people were buried with many of their belongings. A man might be buried with his sword and the tools of his trade. A woman would need her craftworking items and perhaps her best clothes and jewellery. As a result, burials have preserved for us some of the finest examples of Viking craftwork.

This gold altar piece (above) shows King Harald Bluetooth being baptised as a Christian. Most Vikings became Christians, but also continued to worship their old gods. The silversmith's mould (right) could be used to make hammers of Thor and Christian crosses.

This small embossed silver cross was found in a grave in Sweden. Beautifully made, it depicts the crucifixion of Jesus Christ.

These carved wooden panels are from a church in Iceland. They are thought to depict the heads of early Christian saints.

24

Eventually, most Vikings were converted to Christianity. In Denmark, King Harald Bluetooth became a Christian in about 975. To show the strength of his new faith, he exhumed (removed) the body of his father from its magnificent pagan burial mound at Jelling (shown in the scene), and had it re-buried in a Christian grave under a new church built there.

The archaeological excavation shows the grave of King Harald Bluetooth's father underneath the surviving medieval church. The first Viking church at Jelling was made of wooden posts and planks, as shown in the main scene.

Near to the church at Jelling stands a runestone, which says:
'King Harald ordered this stone to be raised in memory of Gorm his father and Thyra his mother. [He was] that Harald who won all Denmark and made all the Danes Christians.'

This parchment (right) shows Fenrir the wolf, an enemy of the gods, and Yggdrasill, a sacred ash tree.

These pendants (below) represent the pagan gods Thor and Freya.

This silver belt mount (above), which is thought to have belonged to King Harald's father Gorm, was found during excavation of the Jelling burials.

Law, Society and Entertainment

ICELAND AD 955

The most powerful Vikings were the kings and chieftains. However, every free Viking could have a say in their local affairs by attending meetings called Things. The Things settled disputes, made local laws and discussed problems. For example, they might try to settle disputes between families which could otherwise lead to bloody feuds.

Everyone was allowed to put forward their point of view. If the law said that a person was guilty, they might be ordered publicly to pay a fine. Or sometimes it was agreed for two people to fight a duel, which could end in one's death. A duel was a social event, with many spectators.

We know the Vikings enjoyed playing board games similar to modern chess or draughts. Below is a beautifully carved wooden board, used to play a game called hnefatafl.

This small bone flute (right) was discovered in Sweden. It was made by hollowing out a sheep's bone. Holes were then drilled so a range of notes could be played on it.

This set of pan pipes (above) was found in England. They are made of boxwood.

Some Viking board games needed a dice, such as these two examples. One is made of walrus ivory, the other of bone.

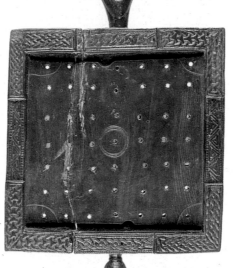

Gaming pieces or counters have been found in many different countries. They are also made from many different materials. Above left are two walrus ivory pieces found in Greenland.

Above is a page of King Harald Finehair's Saga. The saga is a history of Viking kings. Harald Finehair was the first king to rule all of Norway, from about 890.

Left is a 'king' player for hnefatafl carved from amber.

The scene on the right shows a meeting of the Althing, which governed Iceland. The Althing's leader, the Lawspeaker, is making a speech while standing on the Lögberg, the Law Rock. In AD 1000 the Lawspeaker proclaimed that all men in Iceland should become Christians. Although King Håkonsson of Norway took control of Iceland in about 1262, we know that meetings were held annually until 1798.

Some people had to travel many kilometres to get even to their regional Thing, so everyone took the chance to meet friends and socialise. They enjoyed watching and taking part in competitive events such as wrestling, horse-riding and skiing. They set up fairs, with many stalls for traders, and listened to tales told by skalds. Skalds were poets who recited poems and stories that were passed from generation to generation. Some of these tales were eventually written down, as the sagas.

L'ANSE AUX MEADOWS

It is written in the sagas that Vikings voyaged as far as North America, led by a warrior called Leif Ericsson. The land they found there they called Vinland. So what evidence is there that the Vikings really were the first Europeans to reach America?

On the right is part of the saga of Eric the Red. It is written on parchment. The saga describes the voyages of adventure and discovery made by brave Viking men and women in their ships. It also tells of the Norsemen's encounters with people called Skraelings. Eric the Red was banished from his homeland for 'some killings', so he and his band of followers made new lives for themselves in Greenland. It was Eric's son Leif who is supposed to have landed in Vinland.

Left is a silver coin minted in the reign of the Viking king, Olaf Kyrre. This coin was excavated at an American Indian site in Maine, USA. How did it get there? Was it traded between the Vikings and the Skraelings?

Above is a bronze pin which was found in the remains of a longhouse at L'Anse aux Meadows.

The main evidence is the discovery at L'Anse aux Meadows in Newfoundland of three longhouses and other buildings alongside a freshwater stream. One is a hut complete with a furnace, which must have been a smith's workplace.

Other evidence, including 90 iron nails, suggests that boats were built or repaired there. In Newfoundland there was an ample supply of wood. Perhaps the settlers took wood to Greenland and Iceland, where there were few trees and so wood was in great demand.

This arrow-head made from quartzite was discovered in a cemetery in Greenland. It is believed to be of native American origin, and to have been brought to Greenland by the Vinland voyagers.

Below is a piece of a small Viking bow, shaped from wood. A wooden bow of the same style has been found in England and dated to the late 10th century.

A few items found on the site would have been used by Vikings. These include a bronze pin with a ring end (actually of Celtic design) and a spindle whorl from a loom. Carbon dating and dendrochronology have confirmed that the site dates from the Viking period.

The sagas say that the Vikings encountered the native inhabitants of the area, who they called 'Skraelings'. At first the Vikings were able to barter with the Skraelings, but later some fighting took place (shown above). However, no burials have been found at L'Anse aux Meadows. This suggests that the settlement was not permanent, but was used by expeditions who stayed for no more than a few years at a time.

The few artefacts of possible Viking origin found at L'Anse aux Meadows include this soapstone spindle whorl (top) and stone lamp (right).

In the peat bog at L'Anse aux Meadows, archaeologists have discovered pieces of worked wood, such as a boat repair patch (centre right). These have been dated by dendrochronology to the Viking Age.

GLOSSARY

This list explains the meaning of some of the words
and terms used in the book.

**HANDLE MADE
OF ANTLER**

**A WOMAN
WITH AN
EMBROIDERED
APRON**

ALTHING	The national government of Iceland.
AMBER	An orange-coloured stone made of fossilised tree sap. It can be polished and used to make jewellery.
ANTLER	The bony horn of a deer.
ARAB	A member of a people who come from countries in the Middle East and North Africa.
ARCHAEOLOGIST	A person who finds and studies the remains of past cultures.
ARTEFACT	An item which has been made by people.
BARTER	Exchanging goods for something other than money.
BRAZIER	A heater, containing burning coal or wood, that can be carried.
BURIAL MOUND	An earth mound in which Vikings buried their dead. Some mounds contained whole Viking ships.
BYZANTINE EMPIRE	The name of the eastern Roman empire after about AD 330.
CARBON DATING	A scientific technique that can date plant and animal samples by the amount of radioactive carbon 14 in them.
CARGO	Goods carried on a boat.
CHRISTIANITY	A religion based on belief in the life, death and teachings of Jesus Christ.
DENDRO-CHRONOLOGY	A method of dating wood from the patterns of a tree's annual growth rings. It can be used to date wood rings accurately to more than 7,000 years ago.
DIRHAM	A type of silver coin used by Arabs.
DRAUGHT	The depth of ship beneath the water when it is floating.
EMBROIDERY	Cloth decorated with sewn patterns and designs.
EMPEROR	The ruler of an empire, usually with more power than a king or queen.
EXCAVATION	A place where soil or other material is removed to reveal the remains of buildings or other objects.
FEUD	A long and bitter quarrel, usually between two families.
FIORD	A long narrow inlet of sea.
FLAX	A type of plant that can be used to make cloth.
FURNACE	A very hot fire, used by smiths to soften metal so it can be bent, shaped or twisted.
HIDE	An animal skin.
HILT	The handle of a sword or dagger.
HYGIENE	Keeping clean and free from germs.
ILLUMINATE	To decorate a book or document with gold or bright colours.
IVORY	A hard white substance like bone.
JARL	A Viking noble or chieftain, a local ruler. The most powerful jarls became kings, ruling whole countries.

QUERN

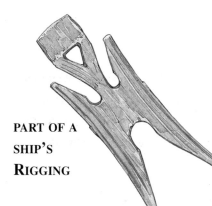

PART OF A
SHIP'S
RIGGING

RUNES ON A
RUNESTONE

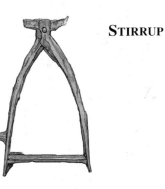

SPINDLE

STIRRUP

KNOT	A nautical mile per hour, about one-and-a-half kilometres per hour.
LONGHOUSE	A Viking home, usually found on farms. Most had one or two rooms. The walls were made of wooden planks, wattle and daub (woven branches covered with clay or mud), or turf.
LOOM	A frame used for weaving (making) cloth.
MONASTERY	A place where monks live and work.
MONK	A man who has undertaken religious vows and usually lives in a monastery with other monks.
MOOR	Race of people of Arab descent, who inhabited regions of North Africa and Spain.
NORSEMEN	Another name for Vikings – 'Northmen'. The Vikings who lived in the area we now call Russia were known as the Rus.
PAGAN	The name given to a person who believes in many gods.
QUERN	Stones used for grinding corn.
RANSOM	A sum of money paid for the release of a prisoner.
REPLICA	A copy or model of an object.
RIGGING	A ship's mast, ropes, blocks and sails.
RUNES	Symbols of an alphabet used by the Vikings, which had 16 symbols. It was only carved on objects, such as bone, wood or stone, never written with pen and ink.
SACRIFICE	An offering, usually to please the gods.
SCUTTLING	The deliberate sinking of a ship or boat.
SKALD	A Viking poet. Many skalds were employed by wealthy kings and chieftains to tell stories of their heroic deeds.
SKRAELINGS	The name, meaning 'screechers' or 'wretches', that Vikings gave to the native inhabitants of the American continent.
SPINDLE	A slender rod used in spinning. A spindle whorl is a weight used to keep the thread straight.
STIRRUP	A foot rest for a person riding a horse.
THING	A national or local assembly of Vikings.
THRALL	A slave. The Vikings seized slaves on raids, or purchased them from foreign traders. Vikings could be made slaves if they became too poor to support themselves.
VARANGIAN GUARD	The bodyguard of the Byzantine Emperor. The Vikings were called Varangians by the Byzantines.

QUOTATIONS

Much of what we know about Viking history and culture comes from the accounts of people who met or saw the Vikings. Al-Tartushi was an Arab traveller who visited Hedeby in the 10th century. He must have found the Viking way of life very different to his own, and believed that the Vikings were rude and uncivilized. Nevertheless he is probably a reliable witness who wrote down what he saw and heard. Some of the accounts of Christian churchmen might not be so reliable. The Church had suffered raids by the most aggressive Vikings, so its members disliked the pagan Norsemen, even if they had not suffered personally.

INDEX